LARRY BURKETT

Giving & Tithing

*Includes Serving
and Stewardship*

MOODY PRESS
CHICAGO

ISBN: 0-8024-3737-0

7 9 10 8 6
Printed in the United States of America

About the Author

Larry Burkett is committed to teaching God's people His principles for managing money. Unfortunately, money management is one area often neglected by Christians, and it is a major cause of conflict and disruption in both business and family life.

For more than two decades Larry has counseled and taught God's principles for finance across the country. As founder and president of Christian Financial Concepts, Larry has counseled, conducted seminars, and written numerous books about finances. In additon, he hosts two of CFC's four radio broadcasts, heard on more than 1,100 radio outlets worldwide.

Giving and Tithing

TOO BUSY TO SERVE

Nothing interferes more with our ability to serve God than our need to earn a living. An observer from one hundred years ago would be awestruck by the "improvement" in our living standard and by the amount of leisure time our technology now provides us. Few North Americans regularly work more than a fifty-hour week; most work forty-four hours or less. In addition, we now live an average of eighteen years longer than we did one hundred years ago and have at least one-third more disposable income per family. When all of those factors are weighed, together with the fact that in America alone there are perhaps twenty million Christians, it seems clear that we ought to be getting out the message of Jesus Christ much better than we are.

The simple truth is that most Americans are too busy to serve God. We have grown complacent and comfortable in God's blessing and have forgotten the first commandment. In the meantime, immorality and cults have grown to alarming proportions because their advocates are more zealous in their support than we are. Since God *asks* for obedience rather than demands it, many Christians simply ignore the very reason for their existence: to glorify God. Without exception, God has a unique and meaningful plan for every believer that does not depend on age, income, or ability.

It is also clear that God calls each of us to fill this gap. Like Esther, every believer must decide either to be used by God or to be bypassed and allow another to be chosen instead. What a loss that we allow temporary comforts and laziness to rob us of true riches, both immediate and eternal!

"Since all these things are to be destroyed in this way, what sort of people ought you to be in holy conduct and godliness" (2 Peter 3:11).

Most Christians would never refuse to do God's will; it's just that the timing is not right. When God calls us, He wants obedience first and worldly wisdom last. We allow the urgent things of our society to overshadow the important things, but that is not unique to our generation. In fact, Christ experienced it in His walk on Earth and predicted it. He told a parable about God calling men to follow Him. They were invited to a dinner, but most were too busy to attend. They wanted to be part of what was happening but had too many responsibilities.

CONSIDER THE COST

Service to Jesus Christ is demanding. It may

actually mean that we have to work as hard for God's kingdom as we do for earthly riches. Few salespeople consider it a great imposition on their time to talk about their product line. Being a success at anything requires dedication, training, and perseverance. It would be a hungry company that trained its salespeople to expect perfect success on every call. Just one turndown and they would all give up, considering themselves failures. Instead, the key to successful sales starts long before the product is seen; in fact, it starts at the job interview. A good sales manager knows that not everybody can be a good salesperson, and many don't even want to be. Christ knew that not everybody would serve God and most might not even want to.

Some want to have a foot in both worlds. They are willing to be called Christians, provided they can pick the times and places to serve. *"Jesus said to him, 'No one, after putting his hand to the plow and looking back, is fit for the kingdom of God'"* (Luke 9:62).

These people are actually worse off as Christians than they were as nonbelievers. They are content to know about God but are fruitless fakers who generate false blessings. They are poorly nourished spiritually and quickly waste away until there is real doubt in their minds about their salvation. *"Other seed fell on rocky soil, and as soon as it grew up, it withered away, because it had no moisture"* (Luke 8:6). They truly fall prey to

6

every wind of doctrine because they are too busy to grow firm roots.

THORNS OF LIFE

"The seed which fell among the thorns, these are the ones who have heard, and as they go on their way they are choked with worries and riches and pleasures of this life, and bring no fruit to maturity" (Luke 8:14).

In the parable of the sower, Christ defines the thorns as worries, riches, and pleasures of this world. At first glance, one could assume that committed service to God would yield peace, but judging from the way Christians avoid total service to God, the peace is bland.

Yet Jesus Christ said that total service to God yields peace and blessings within His will: *"For all these things the nations of the world eagerly seek; but your Father knows that you need these things. But seek for His kingdom, and these things shall be added to you"* (Luke 12:30-31).

Each of us has experienced the thorns of this world. Everything around us is moving at a frantic pace. A family can hardly get one car paid off before another is needed. Only twenty-five years ago our goal was a high school education to get a good job; now it's a college degree. Family life is degraded because it now takes both spouses working to hang on to the "good life."

GOOD WORKS

Just as misguided are Christians who apply themselves to fruitless effort in the name of the Lord. They busy themselves to the point of exhaustion, going to conferences and countless church activities and serving on committees. They rarely, if ever, quiet themselves enough for the Lord to direct them. They are irritable and often envious of others. They are working *at* God's work but not *in* it. Even those who walked with Christ suffered from this busy malady from time to time.

Once when Jesus was visiting Martha's home, she complained that she was stuck doing all the work while Mary just sat and listened to Jesus. Jesus told Martha, *"You are worried and bothered about so many things; but only a few things are necessary, really only one, for Mary has chosen the good part, which shall not be taken away from her"* (Luke 10:41-42).

Many Christians have taken on a life of meaningless works to avoid the reality of serving God according to His will. The fruits of true service (see Galatians 5:22-23) cannot be denied, whereas the effects of human work cannot be hidden.

If you wonder how to determine if one's service was truly being blessed by the Lord, you might ask that person's pastor or close friends. However, the best and by far the most enlightening is to ask his or her family.

SOWING AND REAPING

Most Christians are familiar with the principle of sowing and reaping as it applies to giving—though few really believe it. That principle applies to sharing time in the Lord's work. Just as God can multiply the fruits of our labor, He also can multiply the use of our time. Any good administrator knows that ten minutes spent in productive effort is more valuable than two hours of confusion and frustration. Therefore one of the first things a busy, frustrated, overworked Christian needs to do is to dedicate the best part of the day, week, month, and year to the Lord. To do so will mean reordering priorities at work and at home and establishing sound goals, but before you do that read Luke 6:38.

GOAL-SETTING

PERSONAL

No other goals are going to be meaningful until the first and most important one is settled—one's relationship with God. In Psalm 51:10-13 David tells us of some prerequisites to teaching others God's way: assurance of salvation, a steadfast spirit, the Holy Spirit's control, and a clean heart. If any of those is missing, utter frustration will result. If a Christian's first priority is God, then an understanding of God's way is mandatory.

That means personal Bible study. It also means a personal prayer life dedicated to the needs of others as well as to personal needs.

FAMILY

Most families drift for lack of a rudder: the father's leadership. A family's most important need is a godly father; that is far more important than all the material possessions a parent can provide.

WORK

There is nothing wrong with being successful, even by worldly standards, unless one becomes a failure by godly standards. The rate of divorce and bankruptcy among Christians is an undeniable indicator that Christians have been duped into using the world's yardstick as their measuring stick. Every Christian must ask, "Am I certain my priorities are in line with God's?" If not, a change is in order, no matter what the cost is in dollars and cents.

Usually those at the highest end of the material scale are the biggest violators of priorities (executives, doctors, attorneys, and so on). But equally guilty are many in full-time Christian service, with pastors leading the group. *It is vain for you to rise up early, to retire late, to eat the bread of painful labors; for He gives to His beloved even in his sleep* (Psalm 127:2).

10

PUTTING GOD FIRST

To some degree, we all suffer from being too busy to serve God. Some are so busy doing things *for* God that they fail to do the things *of* God. Some have already been called by God to go into full-time Christian service, but they weigh the call against the cost and decide they can serve God better where they are. Others clutter their lives with so much materialism that they never have time to listen to God. The urgent things crowd out the important things, and Christian service is shelved until "a better time."

We can all give thanks to those committed saints, from the apostles on down, who did not think that fame and success in the eyes of men were as important as God's blessings. One day each of us will evaluate success on the basis of Christ's evaluation and none other. I trust that each of us will hear Him say, "Well done, My good and faithful servant" (see Matthew 25:21).

SEEK THE KINGDOM

"Seek first His kingdom and His righteousness; and all these things shall be added to you" (Matthew 6:33). The Lord admonishes us to seek first His kingdom instead of worrying about material possessions. There has never been a generation of Christians so caught up in worry about possessions as we are. We have a greater abundance

available on a daily basis than any previous generation. Most of us have machines that reduce our daily household labor, our children are well-clothed and well-educated, and life expectancy is beyond God's promise of three-score and ten. We have insurance plans, retirement plans, disability plans, and unemployment plans. Yet we are so caught up in making more money and buying bigger and better things that we have lost our focus on the unsaved world. God's Word keeps asking us the same question: Are we seeking first the kingdom of God?

WHAT DO YOU STAND FOR?

It seems evident that since we will spend eternity in the presence of God and live only seventy years or so on this earth, we should be more concerned about what we will receive then than what we are getting now. But when we review our priorities, it is apparent that most Christians live without real hope, as Paul describes it in Romans 8:24-25. We're willing to settle for what we can see, rather than what is unseen. That is exactly the principle that Christ is teaching in Matthew 6:19-33.

Material things are not what cause our difficulties. God says that He will give us the things that the world cherishes so much. But are we more dedicated to accumulating material things than to serving God? The evidence shows that we are serving money—not God. *"Where your treasure is, there will your heart be also"* (Matthew 6:21).

The question is often asked, "What do Christians stand for?" The answer the world would give is, "Not much other than what we do." The sad part is that most people really want to know a personal God. We have the only hope for a world without hope; yet we spend our time pursuing vain things.

ONLY TWO CHOICES

Christ says that we have only two choices: to follow God or to follow money.

"No one can serve two masters; for either he will hate the one and love the other, or he will hold to one and despise the other. You cannot serve God and mammon" (Matthew 6:24).

The scriptural warning is clear: We will be judged on the evidence of our material lives. The attraction of materialism is so great that Christ devoted two-thirds of His parables to warning His disciples about it. The writers of the Epistles amplified that teaching as they observed the destructive force of materialism in the lives of believers.

"The love of money is a root of all sorts of evil, and some by longing for it have wandered away from the faith, and pierced themselves with many a pang" (1 Timothy 6:10).

Again, it's not material things that are the

problem; it is materialism. What is alarming about our generation is that we have found a way to scripturally rationalize our excesses. Many Christians actually believe that we can attract the unsaved by having the best. Let me assure you that those who are seriously seeking God are not attracted by luxuries. They are attracted by an uncompromising commitment to God. If that commitment also yields material blessings, it's just an added benefit.

GIVE, AND IT WILL BE GIVEN TO YOU

"Give, and it will be given to you; good measure, pressed down, shaken together, running over, they will pour into your lap. For by your standard of measure it will be measured to you in return" (Luke 6:38). Few Scripture verses are quoted more often than that verse regarding the principle of giving and receiving. When I first read the verse, shortly after committing my life to Christ, I pondered it for many weeks. Did God really mean what that verse says? Do God's promises depend on our giving first? I read the previous and subsequent verses to see if perhaps it could be interpreted in another context. I then studied parallel and contrasting verses. After dedicating many hours to God's Word, I concluded that I really didn't understand the meaning of Luke 6:38. There were some obvious difficulties

with the principle that receiving was a matter of giving first. What about Christians who give but don't receive much in return?

My first response was to assume that the principle did not apply to all Christians. Perhaps it applied only to those with a gift of giving. I quickly eliminated that rationale. If Luke 6:38 applies to only a select few, Christ would not have delivered the message in Luke 6 to the masses. God may select a few to receive and dispose of a large amount of His resources, but the principle described in this verse is a promise to anyone who will apply it.

Then I thought that perhaps the principle applies to spiritual rather than material rewards. Indeed, further study confirmed that it does apply to spiritual rewards. But there is no way to dissociate the material giving and receiving, since in verses 30-35 Christ makes direct reference to material things. The more I reviewed other Scripture dealing with the principle of giving and receiving, the more I realized there was no contradiction at all.

OBSERVATIONS

Once an understanding of God's promise is reached, it is necessary to believe that promise. I determined to make a study of giving and receiving in the lives of Christians I knew and then match the result of my study to God's Word. Since all of God's principles are given as examples for living, an applied principle must be verified in changed lives. If it isn't, we're probably misunderstanding the principle or else not applying it. Before I define the scriptural principle, I will give some observations of the study that started many years ago and still continues.

1. Most Christians give far less than one-tenth of their income to work done in the Lord's name.

2. Many Christians give at least one tenth of their incomes regularly but do not experience what they assess to be God's material or spiritual bounty.

3. Many Christians give at least a tenth of their incomes and can identify many instances of God's abundance, either materially, spiritually, or both.

4. A small percentage of Christians give far beyond a tenth of their incomes but cannot identify anything they would describe as God's abundant return.

5. A very small percentage of Christians give far beyond a tenth of their incomes and can identify God's response, both generally and specifically.

Of course, there were other categories and instances in which Christians moved from one group to another. Many of those can be explained because of spiritual growth or withdrawal, which obviously affects every area of our lives. A few can be classified as unique from a biblical perspective. That is most clear when a spiritually mature Christian gives in great abundance and outwardly appears to suffer materially. The apostle Paul would most assuredly identify with that group. God has a separate and unique plan for such people, and the depth of their commitment to Christ sets them apart in spiritual blessings. I offer some observations about these groups, with no intent to be judgmental. I believe God has provided us with material indicators of spiritual conditions. They are not for accusation but for admonition.

DON'T ROB GOD

Those who give less than a tenth of their income limit what God can do for them according to His own Word. *"Will a man rob God? Yet you are robbing Me! But you say, 'How have we robbed Thee?' In tithes and offerings"* (Malachi 3:8). Lest we somehow believe that principle applies only to the Old Covenant, Paul amplifies it for us: *"Now this I say, he who sows sparingly shall also reap sparingly; and he who sows bountifully shall also reap bountifully."* (2 Corinthians 9:6). A lack of giving is an external material indicator that spiritual changes need to be made.

Those who give more than a tenth, but not sacrificially, may experience God's abundance according to His plan for them because they are meeting God's prerequisites for them at that time.

Many who give what we consider a material abundance and do not experience any particular spiritual or material reply may actually be giving

17

for self-motivated reasons. Many people try to bribe God into blessing them. They are like Simon in Acts 8, who when he observed the benefits of God's power tried to acquire it without meeting the spiritual prerequisites. They demand God's blessing to reward what they consider to be their sacrifice. They are not in subjection to God but are trying to exercise control over Him. Paul addressed that attitude also in Romans 11:34-35: *"Who has known the mind of the Lord, or who became His counselor? Or who has first given to Him that it might be paid back to him again?"*

BELIEVE GOD

Another group is made up of those who give, expecting but never demanding. Although God often returns far beyond their expectations both materially and spiritually, their giving is out of a desire to please God, not a desire to profit. The evidence can be found in the fact that usually their sacrificial giving comes long before God responds, and their giving far exceeds their accumulation, regardless of the supply.

A Christian friend in Atlanta exemplifies that principle clearly. I met him several years ago, during a particularly difficult time in his financial circumstances. He'd been totally committed to giving sacrificially to God's kingdom, had experienced great blessings, and in fact was noted in Christian circles as a giver. Then for an extended period of time the bounty was withdrawn, and for all intents and purposes he was broke. His Christian "Job's friends" quickly pointed out every character flaw he had and advised him to repent and get straight with God. After much soul-searching, prayer, and fasting, he concluded he was where God wanted him to be, doing what God wanted him to do. Consequently, he and his wife decided to give more, not less.

Mark 11:24 says, *"Therefore I say to you, all things for which you pray and ask, believe that you have received them, and they shall be granted you."* He concluded that in order to believe, he had to act. So they began to give furniture and other things they had collected during the abundance to others who had greater needs.

Now God is using him to supply enormous sums of money to His work. His love for giving is matched by a deep sensitivity to the needs of others, and there is never a doubt who gets the glory for the abundance.

Several times he and his wife have saved enough to build a new home, and each time they have given the money away to meet a need in God's work. Every time I see him he is excited about making more money so they can give more away. The only caution I have ever given this kind of giver is not to give away all of the "seed corn."

The spiritual principle behind Luke 6:38 is indeed giving and receiving, but it is not giving to receive. The prerequisites to receiving are found in Luke 6:27-37. A Christian who lives by these principles practices the surrendered life. Therefore, giving is simply a material expression of the deeper spiritual obedience to Christ. Nearly every Christian desires to be obedient to God, and in many ways most are. However, Christ warned us that the greatest threat to our walk with God is the tug of our materialistic world.

"The one on whom seed was sown among the thorns, this is the man who hears the word, and the worry of the world, and the deceitfulness of riches choke the word, and it becomes unfruitful" (Matthew 13:22).

WHY GIVE TO GOD?

The main reason we should give to God is really for our own sakes. In so doing we remember that He is the owner of all we have, and we are only managers. When we try keeping it all to ourselves, we reveal a serious problem in our perspective. When we view money and possessions as belonging to us, we inevitably begin to look at every other aspect of our lives the same way. We see ourselves as being in charge. We begin to think of God as our servant, existing solely to help us from time to time when we call Him. Instead, we must remember that we are God's servants, always ready to do His will. That is why we call Him Lord; He is our Ruler, Owner, Sovereign, and King.

That is why giving to God is so important. It reminds us who He is, who we are, and what our relationship should be to the things He has allowed us to manage in His name. Giving must be done in love, with a thankful and willing heart, all the time recognizing God as the owner of everything. Haggai 2:8 says, *"The silver is Mine, and the gold is Mine, declares the Lord of hosts."* And Deuteronomy 8:18 says, *"But you shall remember the Lord your God, for it is He who is giving you power to make wealth."*

There are a number of good reasons to give, but there are also many poor ones. Let's look at the good reasons first.

GOOD REASONS

1. Giving should be an outward, material expression of a deep spiritual commitment, an indication of a willing and obedient heart. (See Malachi 3:8; James 1:22; 1 John 3:17.)

2. We should give out of grateful hearts and with an attitude of joy. *"Let each one do just as he has purposed in his heart; not grudgingly or under compulsion; for God loves a cheerful giver."* (2 Corinthians 9:7).

3. Some may have the spiritual gift of giving described in Romans 12:8. These people live disciplined lives, which enables them to give generously. They are especially sensitive to the needs of others and conscious of the need to check out every cause

to which they give. Generally, they are prudent people.

4. You may give out of conviction. Perhaps the Holy Spirit is prompting you to give to a special cause. How can you determine if such a desire to give is actually from God or just an emotional response? Read God's Word and pray. If you are married, include your spouse in the decision to ensure balance in your giving.

BAD REASONS

Now let's examine wrong reasons to give.

1. Giving for the express purpose of receiving does not please God. Many people try to bribe God by giving to Him first. They quote Luke 6:38 as their reference. It is true that God will spiritually and physically bless those who give—but only when our motive is right and we are giving out of a sincere desire to please Him. Remember, God looks at the heart. An example of giving to get can be found in the story of Simon (Acts 8), who offered money to the apostles for the ability to bestow the Holy Spirit by laying his hands on others. The offer brought a stern rebuke from Peter, who advised Simon to repent and ask God for forgiveness: *"Who has first given to Him that it might be paid back to him again?"* (Romans 11:35).

2. Some give out of fear. Reverence for and respect toward God, when tempered with confidence in His love, are signs of spiritual maturity.

That is not the kind of fear I am referring to. What I warn against is giving because someone told you that if you don't give God will punish you. For example, illness can motivate Christians to give out of fear—so that God will make them well. If you give because you feel intimidated, you are giving under compulsion, which is contrary to God's Word (see 2 Corinthians 9:7). Never support a ministry that uses threats as a fund-raising gimmick.

3. Giving to impress others does not impress God. The Pharisees of Christ's time had this problem. Jesus told them, *"When you give alms, do not let your left hand know what your right hand is doing"* (Matthew 6:3).

People who have a problem with pride need to do their giving modestly and humbly. That doesn't mean that all giving must be done entirely in secret. It would be difficult for Christian ministries to prepare yearly budgets if they didn't have an idea of how much to expect from their supporters, so letting a ministry know that you will contribute a certain amount each year is helpful. But we are not to draw attention to ourselves when we give.

Allowing your children to witness your giving, particularly when sacrifice is involved, will teach them the importance of commitment. Giving for applause or approval, however, is unscriptural.

HOW DO I GIVE?

1. Give out of your abundance according to the principle taught in 2 Corinthians 8:14. God doesn't want you to give until you are made poor, unless it is to improve your spiritual life. A balanced attitude toward material things can be found in Proverbs 30:8-9. God's main concern is your heart.

2. Commitment is an important ingredient in giving, but confusion exists when it comes to distinguishing between faith promises and pledges. A faith promise is a commitment to give a certain amount, which allows ministries to prepare good, logical financial planning for the year. It is understood that if God doesn't provide the funds you're not obligated to give them. A pledge, on the other hand, is an absolute commitment to pay something. This type of giving is presumptuous, whereas a faith promise is scriptural (Hebrews 11:1).

3. Not all giving consists of cash donations. You may donate your time or services or noncash gifts, such as food, furniture, and clothing. Avoid giving useless or junk gifts. You also may give something with an appreciated value (an asset you bought at a low price that is now worth much more). In this category might be stocks, bonds, jewelry, real estate, or anything that increases in value.

4. Some organizations encourage people to

borrow to give. I do not believe that is scriptural. It doesn't require much trust to borrow money. Deuteronomy 15:4-6 says that if we obey and trust God, we will not have to borrow money. There is no example in Scripture of God ever using a loan to manifest His will in the lives of His people.

5. Sacrificial giving is a way to honor God but, once again, it should be the result of a good attitude, not a desire to impress others. All of us have been called to suffer for Christ according to Philippians 1:29. In today's generation that may not include great physical sacrifice, but it does require an understanding that the purpose of our abundance is to further the kingdom of God. Neither a voluntary rejection of all wealth nor a display of material success is evidence of a balanced Christian walk. In this country, however, few of us have a problem with sacrificing too much.

THE PRINCIPLE OF NEW TESTAMENT GIVING

For the majority of Christians, serving God will never lead to worldwide fame, writing best-selling books, or singing before thousands. But regardless of the work to which we're called, few Christians really cannot afford to give, and when giving is done in love, it exemplifies the greatest sacrifice ever made for mankind—the death of Jesus on the cross.

Jesus gave out of love when He left heaven and equality with God to come to Earth. It was because of love that He became a servant and gave His life to save us from our sins. And the Bible tells us that God was motivated by love when He gave His only begotten Son.

THE MACEDONIANS

Unlike the early Christians, most of us aren't faced with the possibility of sacrificing our lives for the Gospel. But we can follow the Christ-like example of the Macedonians, who not only gave out of love but loved to give.

One instance of their giving is related by the apostle Paul: *"Now, I am going to Jerusalem serving the saints. For Macedonia and Achaia have been pleased to make a contribution for the poor among the saints in Jerusalem. Yes, they were pleased to do so, and they are indebted to them. For if the Gentiles have shared in their spiritual things, they are indebted to minister to them also in material things"* (Romans 15:25–27). The message of the gospel had gone out to the Macedonians from Jerusalem. In return, they showed their love for the poor saints in Jerusalem by giving to meet their needs.

That attitude can be seen in another passage about the Macedonians (2 Corinthians 8:1-5), who not only gave sacrificially but actually begged for an opportunity to give. Paul reveals in verses 3-4, *"According to their ability, and beyond their ability they gave of their own accord, begging us with much entreaty for the favor of participation in the support of the saints."*

WHERE TO BEGIN

The key to such giving is revealed by Paul in verse 5: *"They first gave themselves to the Lord and to us by the will of God."*

Once Christians have gone beyond the first step of giving themselves to the Lord, they are in a position to give their possessions in love. Why? Because they have yielded their will to the God of love, who is working in and through them for the benefit of others. Thus, giving begins with surrendering to God.

A MODEL GIVER

An example of the proper attitude in giving—love for God, not money—is found in the life of C. T. Studd, a Christian world champion cricket player in the 1800s. When Studd's father died, Studd inherited 29,000 pounds, equal to about $150,000 at that time. It would be a sizeable amount even by today's standards.

But not wanting to "clutter up" his life, Studd decided to invest his money with God. He sent 5,000 pounds to Hudson Taylor, who organized the China Inland Mission; 5,000 to William Booth, founder of the Salvation Army; and 5,000 to D. L. Moody to start a work in India. Although Moody didn't go to India, the money was used to start Moody Bible Institute.

After completing all of his giving, Studd had only 3,400 pounds left, which he gave to his wife on their wedding day. Her response: "The rich young ruler was asked to give His all." So they sent the remaining money to General Booth—anonymously.

Tithing

A DEFINITION

The tithe serves as an external, material testimony of God's ownership of the material and spiritual things of our lives. The first place God's Word mentions the tithe is Genesis 14. On his return from the daring rescue of Lot from four enemy kings, Abraham encountered the priest Melchizedek and voluntarily surrendered to him a tithe (one-tenth) of everything he had.

The word *tithe* in Hebrew is *maaser* and in Greek *dekate*. It literally means "tenth." After the word appears in Genesis it occurs twenty-eight times in the Old Testament. It appears in two references in the New Testament: in Matthew 23:23 and in Hebrews 7, where it describes Abraham's relationship to Christ by drawing a parallel between Abraham's tithe and his acknowledgment of God's sovereignty.

IS TITHING LEGALISM?

Although the tithe is mentioned in the law, no punishment was indicated for not tithing. There is a consequence (the loss of blessings), but there is *no* punishment from God for not tithing. The rewards of tithing are described in Malachi 3:10-11, where God promises to pour out a blessing and keep the devourer away. Tithing should always be a voluntary act on the part of God's people.

THE PROMISE OF THE TITHE

Although not tithing may cause a withholding of God's blessings, tithing with proper motives invokes God's blessings.

"'Bring the whole tithe into the storehouse, so that there may be food in My house, and test Me now in this,' says the Lord of hosts, 'if I will not open for you the windows of heaven, and pour out for you a blessing until it overflows. Then I will rebuke the devourer for you, so that it may not destroy the fruits of the ground; nor will your vine in the field cast its grapes,' says the Lord of hosts. 'And all the nations will call you blessed for you shall be a delightful land,' says the Lord of hosts" (Malachi 3:10-12).

PURPOSE OF THE TITHE

Was the tithe intended to help establish the physical church and pay the wages of "full-time" ministers? If so, it took a long time for the word to get around, because it was not until Moses was given the law that the tithe filled this need.

No, the tithe was established as a physical,

earthly demonstration of man's commitment to God. God understood our greedy, selfish nature and provided an identifiable sign of our sincerity. By surrendering some of our physical resources, we testify to our origin, just as a farmer does when he surrenders some of his crop back to the earth from which it came.

To verify this purpose, it is necessary to go back to Malachi. Malachi was a prophet sent by God to confront His people with the fact that they had turned from Him. As could be expected, they denied it. They thought God had deserted them, for they claimed to be obeying Him. But they worshiped only when it was convenient. They gave to God, but their gifts were sick and blemished. They gave only for social or ceremonial purposes.

But Malachi struck to the heart of the issue when he asked, "Will a man rob God?" They denied it saying, "How have we robbed Thee?" The evidence was presented in the fact that God's storehouse was not full.

The people were suffering with meager provisions, affliction on every side, lack of leadership, and disunity. How did God indicate their real problem? Their lack of giving proved they had turned away from their source of blessing. Giving the tithe is the outward sign of inner commitment. It is material surrender prompted by spiritual surrender.

Thus God said the tithe is an expression of

commitment (or lack of it) by which we can determine our relationship to Him. It was never intended that we should all give the same, but we should give according to our abundance and our convictions. The tenth was considered the minimum.

The story of Job is a clear and striking reminder that no one, no matter how powerful, has a permanent hold on anything in this world. Suddenly stripped of his many possessions, Job pointed to his mortality as the undeniable evidence of God's controlling ownership: *"Naked I came from my mother's womb, and naked I shall return there. The Lord gave and the Lord has taken away"* (1:21).

When done for the right reason, tithing is the confirmation of God's controlling ownership, which means we simply manage what He has entrusted to us. Yet, many Christians seem to ignore the facts and cling to their money as if it were theirs for eternity.

TEN PERCENT?

How much should Christians tithe, and is tithing enough?

There are several additional offerings described as the "tithes of your increase" in Deuteronomy. These were special offerings meant to care for the priests, the poor, the sick, and the elderly. It is not possible to come up with an amount, but I calculate these total "regular" gifts to be approximately 23 percent per year. That excludes nonregular gifts to meet specific needs. Today it would be the equivalent of a family's committed giving. God may convict you to give to special needs beyond your regular giving.

A family that finds itself unable to make a commitment of a tenth of its resources to God should realistically examine its spending and living habits. Perhaps that will require a critical examination of spiritual values as well. If more funds were needed for family conveniences, the average family would somehow find the means to buy what they wanted. For budgeting tips see *Personal Finances* (Moody 1998).

God never intended for everyone to give the same amount or in the same way, but each should give bountifully and cheerfully (2 Corinthians 9:6–7). The tithe is a testimony of God's ownership; thus, it is meant to be individualized.

Deuteronomy 14:23 says, *"You shall eat in the presence of the Lord your God, at the place where He chooses to establish His name, the tithe of your grain, your new wine, your oil, and the first-born of your herd and your flock, in order that you may learn to fear the Lord your God always."*

WHERE SHOULD MY TITHE GO?

THE STOREHOUSE

In order to bring our tithes into the "storehouse," it is necessary to determine what, exactly, the storehouse is. In biblical times it was a physical place where the Jews delivered their offerings of grain or animals. A storehouse had specific functions according to God's Word.

1. To feed the tribe of Levi (Numbers 18:24-29). The priests and the tribe of Levi would be the equivalent of pastors, church staff, missionaries, and evangelists today. The Levites were the overseers of the storehouse (as far as we know), but the contributions were strictly designated as to use. Some food was always available to care for the poor and the sick so that no one would ever starve.

2. To feed the Hebrew widows and orphans living in the Hebrew city (Deuteronomy 14:28-29). That would be equivalent to the widows and orphans served in a local church.

3. To feed the Gentile poor living in the Hebrew city (Deuteronomy 14:28-29). Today's equivalent would be the unsaved people in the community surrounding a local church.

THE CHURCH

Apparently this system was modified slightly but kept nearly intact in the early church. In Acts 4 we are told that the congregation acted as one unit, selling what was necessary and delivering the proceeds to the apostles to be distributed. Later, under the burden of the growing church, deacons were appointed to ease the burden of distribution.

It is often stated that our modern churches are the storehouses described in the Old Testament and inferred in the New, so our tithes should simply be given to the church. I wish that were true. Few churches today truly operate as storehouses, providing for the needs of the sick, elderly, and orphaned, as well as supporting the inspired teachers of the Word outside of the organized church. Therefore, to the extent that a church lacks in a specific area of ministry, a portion of the tithe should be given to individuals or parachurch organizations that are "filling in the gap."

Many churches are isolated by denominational barriers. They are jealous of each other and content to abdicate physical needs to the government. This is not a condemnation but, rather, an indictment. Most churches have not done so purposefully; they have done it by indifference.

If other people are willing to take our responsibilities, we usually let them.

Now we all suffer accordingly. Satan has slowly inoculated us against the suffering of others, just as he has given the world small doses of religion to inoculate it against Christianity.

CHANGING FINANCIAL DIRECTION

Most Christians who are fearful of tithing, or giving generously to the Lord's work, use the excuse of being strapped financially. Many are in debt or have undertaken unnecessary financial obligations that put them in bondage. Getting out of debt is not only scriptural, with many benefits in its own right, but doing so allows Christians to contribute to the needs of the saints and evangelize the world.

The following testimonies contradict the claim that if you are in debt you cannot afford to give to God abundantly. If Christians who are not wealthy can radically change financial direction, how much more can richly blessed Christians give to God!

Ed and Sarah never had a large income or enjoyed much material wealth. But that didn't stop them from enjoying life or tithing.

One reason for their happiness was Ed's obedience to God. He was a blessing not only to Sarah but to many others as well, because he followed God's plan for his finances and put God first in his life and budget.

In past years, Ed and Sarah had worked in a Teen Challenge ministry for $50 per week, plus room and board. He had taught in a Christian school for $10,000 per year. And he'd worked in a factory at minimum wage. In other words, for many years of their life together, they had hovered near the "poverty level."

However lean the times, though, they faithfully paid their tithe and supported various ministries on a monthly basis. And God honored their faithfulness.

Although they didn't have a new car, their '82 Toyota was paid for on the same day they left the dealership, not after years of monthly payments. Their home furnishings weren't exclusive, but none of them were financed. And although they didn't wear stylish clothes, none of their clothes had been purchased on credit.

Unlike other couples, Ed and Sarah had known times when a Coke was a treat and a salad bar was a luxury. But more important to Sarah was the fact that they were always home to eat their meals together as a family.

One of the greatest examples of God's faithfulness in Ed's and Sarah's lives involved the purchase of their house. They had searched for months to find a suitable house in the $20,000 to $25,000 range but had never felt God's "okay" about making a purchase. After showing Ed and Sarah a very run-down house, which they declined, the real estate agent said, "Oh, by the way, there is a house up for closed bids, with a minimum bid of $13,000. Would you like to see it?"

Ed and Sarah agreed, and as they were walking through the door of the house, the Lord impressed Ed to bid a certain amount. He followed God's direction and was able to buy the house for $18,000. It had recently been on the market at $25,000.

Although it was an older house, it was well-built and in a good neighborhood. By paying extra on the principal, Ed and Sarah paid off the fifteen-year loan in thirty-two months! Again, God was faithful, moving Ed into a construction job that increased his hourly wage from $7 to $12, which allowed them to make the increased principal payments. "Ed was faithful to God in the little things, and God certainly honors His Word," Sarah said. "The construction job will likely play out in a few months, but you know what Jesus said about the sparrows and the lilies! Our trust must never be placed in any *thing*—only in Him, the source of all we need!"

In her seventy-one years Mary had seen plenty of hard times. During the Great Depression her husband, John, had been a young adult, and she had been a teenager. Thus, both had learned how to manage money—a necessary skill in those days.

As senior citizens, Mary and John were still in the money-managing business. Living on $10,000 a year, they planted a half-acre garden, and Mary filled her twenty-five cubic foot freezer with everything she could get her hands on. She was also alert to new ideas for saving money. "My mother taught me a great principle: Watch the dimes, and the dollars will take care of themselves," Mary said.

Recently John and Mary gave $4,000 of their

$10,000 income to the Lord's work. In addition, they bought supplies for their church. And they were still able to put a small amount into savings. When Mary totaled her car, she and John were able to pay cash for a well-running, used automobile.

"One cannot outgive God!" Mary said. "We had all we needed and a few extras. Oh, that God's people might live simply and find the joy of giving much to the Lord!"

Donna and Barry attended their first Christian Financial Concepts seminar in 1984. Donna attended in great frustration because her husband had always handled their money, and prior to her marriage her father had taken care of her finances. So in her opinion, the seminar would be boring and of no value; finances were "for the men."

She was mistaken. At the seminar she hung on to every word, and time slipped by quickly. Afterward, she and Barry were convinced that God was leading them to pay off their house. They had always lived on a budget and had just made some modifications, but their mortgage was looming over them.

Donna and Barry had been involved in ministry since their marriage in 1972. In her opinion, the Lord had always taken care of them and blessed them because Barry was committed to tithing from his gross income.

After the seminar, they trusted God to help them pay off their house, if possible, within five years. Sticking to their plan, they became totally debt free in August 1989.

"Boy, did we celebrate" Donna exclaimed. "What a wonderful feeling of freedom. We realize that there is no way *we* accomplished this task. It had to have been the Lord honoring our obedience to His command in our lives.

"On paper it should not have been possible for a family of four and the years of ministry service we had put in. But God is faithful and did free us. As the Lord continues to free our finances, we give to His work!"

For Allen and Linda, the words of the apostle Paul in Philippians 4:19 were more than a message of encouragement for the first-century church. They represent a personal testimony of God's ability to supply the needs of His children in this century as well.

Each year there was a faith missions conference at Allen and Linda's church. During one of those conferences, God led Allen to give a specific amount to missions each week. He was paid weekly, but that amount was equal to what his family was spending on a weekly basis for food.

In addition, he and Linda had five children, ranging in age from three to fifteen. "I started giving to missions, knowing that we could not afford it," Allen said. "But I also believed God told me to." For fifty-two weeks he continued his giving, and his family never went hungry.

During that time, unsaved men at work suddenly began giving food to Allen, even though neither he nor his wife had told anyone that they were in need. God also provided him with a year's supply of honey, which he used as a sugar substitute because he had diabetes.

The first winter after Allen and Linda made their commitment to missions, the family was supplied with coats and most of the other garments they needed. Some time later they took stock of their clothes, and each of the children had two good coats. So they gave away several coats to other children in need.

By the following summer, Allen and Linda were giving food away themselves. "There were a number of times when all we had for food was $3. Experience has proved my pastor right. Pay your tithe, then your promises to God, then your bills, and let Him take care of the rest," Allen said.

One week in particular, God gave a special blessing to Allen. His middle child, Hannah, was turning eight and for her birthday she wanted a girl's, blue, twenty-inch bicycle with a white basket. The bike was around $70. All Allen could afford was the basket. But a few days before Hannah's birthday a friend called and wanted to know if the family would be interested in a girl's bike. "I went and looked at it, and it wasn't just any girl's bike; it was a blue girl's bike minus the basket," said Allen. "So the Lord had done it again."

Allen got paid on Thursday, and Hannah's party was planned for Saturday. By then all that was left of his paycheck was $3 for food—not enough to buy ice cream and cake. On Friday Allen went to work, and at the end of his shift he found a sack of food in his car. "This was late April. God had been doing this for six months. I didn't even look to see what it was. When I got home, my wife started putting it away, and in the sack was a cake mix with a package of frosting!"

Further evidence of God's blessing involved Allen's car. Because he drove fifty miles each way to work, reliable transportation wasn't an option; it was a must. He and Linda spent several weeks in prayer about a car before buying one. With five children to carry around, Linda wanted a big wagon. Allen wanted a vehicle with good gas mileage that would be easy to work on. In the end, he paid $700 for an '81 station wagon with 140,000 miles on it. After the wagon crossed the 200,000-mile mark, Allen and a Christian brother painted it for $75. Then he took it on a 2,000-mile trip to visit his in-laws. It ran beautifully!

Eventually, Allen went from third shift at work to second shift, which meant Linda needed a car of her own. Again, the couple prayed. The following day at work, during break, he picked up a newspaper and spotted an '80 station wagon with 97,000 miles for sale in the classifieds.

When Allen called about the car, an elderly woman answered the phone. She informed him that the vehicle hadn't run properly and had been sitting for three years. "I asked what was wrong, and she said the carburetor was messed up," Allen explained. "Of all the mechanical things I've done, the only thing I ever specialized in was carburetors."

The family drove twenty miles to look at the car, and in about two hours Allen had it running. The body and tires were in good shape, and Linda now had a station wagon of her own—all for the incredible price of $250!

IMPROVE GIVING IN THE CHURCH

Wouldn't it be great to see God's people open their hearts and give the way they should? We have enough money in North America to fund all the Christian work in the world if the people would just give!

Unfortunately large numbers of North Americans are in financial bondage, and many of those people are Christians. In fact, some Christians are so deeply in debt that if God came down and said, "I want to perform a miracle and lead all of India to Christ through you," they'd have to say, "Lord, come back and see me in eighty years when I'm out of debt."

The tragedy is that the church has literally become shackled because money needed for ministry is tied up in large monthly payments. And the material things those payments are buying don't bring true happiness. By making finances a part of their overall ministry, pastors could help turn this tide of materialism. As church members become financially free, they can encourage others to do the same, and they'll have a greater and greater abundance from which to serve the Lord.

WELFARE

A DEFINITION

Welfare. Whose responsibility is it? Americans view it as a function of government. As a consequence the church, which God made responsible for the administration of welfare, rarely practices it. In 2 Corinthians 9:13 Paul says, *Because of the proof given by this ministry they will glorify God.* That is the purpose of welfare in the church today.

The function of welfare is feeding people and caring for their needs, but the purpose of welfare is drawing people to God by allowing them to see a physical expression of love Christians have for each other and for other people.

Obviously the government's goal in welfare is not to bring people to God. So it really should not be a government function to control, administer, or distribute welfare. Welfare is the function of the body of Christ. The sooner we realize that and are willing to do something about it, the sooner others will come back to God.

There is a great deal of talk about a revival today. We should remember that many revivals start when the body of Christ is practicing Christianity and others are drawn to it.

Every member of a local church should be able to see the fellowship he or she attends as an extension of God's provision. We should feel the freedom to stand up and share our financial needs as freely as we would our physical or spiritual needs.

THE CHURCH'S RESPONSIBILITY

Welfare within the church really does not exist to any significant degree today. The number of churches that have thorough church benevolence programs—meaning they counsel couples with financial needs, provide them with work projects and income, and, if needed, goods and services—is so small that it is almost inconsequential.

But the body of Christ, not the government, should be involved in welfare. The government fails to distinguish the greedy from the needy because its welfare is a political program to gain votes. But God said truly needy people are the church's responsibility. The way a local church handles its money is a visible indicator of its true spiritual condition.

As illustrated in the Bible, we will be held accountable on the day of judgment for our attitude toward the needy.

"Then He will also say to those on His left, 'Depart from Me, accursed ones, into the eternal fire which has been prepared for the devil and his angels; for I was hungry, and you gave Me nothing to eat; I was thirsty, and you gave Me nothing to drink; I was a stranger, and you did not invite Me in; naked, and you did not clothe Me; sick, and in prison, and you did not visit Me.' Then they themselves also will answer, saying, 'Lord, when did we see You hungry, or thirsty, or a stranger, or naked, or sick, or in prison, and did not take care of You?' Then He will answer them, saying, 'Truly I say to you, to the extent that you did not do it to one of the least of these, you did not do it to Me.' And these will go away into eternal punishment, but the righteous into eternal life" (Matthew 25:41–46).

BENEVOLENCE MINISTRY IN YOUR CHURCH

THE BENEVOLENCE COMMITTEE

Before practicing welfare, churches should first be careful to meet a number of prerequisites, including the establishment of a benevolence committee. Three members of the committee should represent three separate gifts: helps, mercy, and administration.

One of the benevolence committee's first jobs should be to develop guidelines for itself, including what kind of assistance will be provided, how much assistance will be provided, and how people will apply for assistance.

The committee can work with other groups in the church that are involved in benevolent activities, such as women's and men's organizations, and perhaps coordinate their activities.

STANDARDS FOR HELPING

Standards for helping, established by the benevolence committee, should include eligibility. God says stewards must be found worthy; so also must people helped by a church benevolence program be found worthy.

In addition, people seeking help must submit to individual counseling. If a couple is seeking help, both the husband and wife should be required to go through financial and spiritual counseling. Simply giving them money won't solve their problems; it will only treat their symptoms.

Often a local church's benevolence program amounts to the pastor simply directing the secretary to write someone a check for food, gas, or rent. However, that's usually the worst thing to do. Without any controls or follow-up, giving money that way is like pouring gasoline on a fire.

People helped by the benevolence committee should be willing to draft a budget plan with the aid of a counselor. Their resource management plan should include a commitment to get out and stay out of debt. Counseling and budgets are necessary, because in about 70 percent of the cases the people in trouble have an adequate supply of money but don't know how to manage it.

A counselor should review the individual's lifestyle and make recommendations without being judgmental. In other words, don't tell a person to sell his or her car, use the proceeds to pay bills, and start riding the bus. Don't make requirements you're not willing to live by yourself. Review the person's lifestyle, and put yourself in his or her position. Ask yourself, "What would I be willing to do?"

A WILLING ATTITUDE

Once a counselor makes recommendations, a person receiving help from the church must be willing to follow them. That's why the benevolence committee must determine an individual's willingness to make necessary changes.

Sometimes people show total unwillingness to make any adjustments. If that's the case, it's time to stop the counseling. No amount of money can help unless they decide to make necessary changes in their lives.

In addition, they must be willing to work.

Some unemployed people are not willing to go to work. They are picky about finding a job that exactly fits their education, personality, and all the rest. But unless they show a willingness to shoulder the responsibility and take a job that is presently available, at least for a short while, they generally are not willing to help themselves. Then the counselor probably needs to say, "I'm sorry. I can't help you any further."

A lack of willingness also may reflect a person's attitude about spiritual training. At Christian Financial Concepts, everyone in financial counseling is required to go through a spiritual education program and receives one of our Bible studies, *How to Manage Your Money*. Everyone is required to do part of this study between each counseling session.

If people haven't done their homework, we don't proceed with the next session. We don't want to be guilty of dealing with the symptom, which is usually financial, and ignoring the problem, because the root problem is almost always spiritual. The spiritual principles they're violating are being reflected through their personal finances.

CON ARTISTS

A lack of willingness may be due to the fact that people are lying about their needs. Some people make a living on handouts and take from the already limited supply of help set aside for truly needy people.

There are some guidelines to follow in determining whether a person seeking help is truly needy.

1. Follow up on stories and details. If that person is telling the truth, he or she will do what is necessary to help verify his or her story.

2. Take time to think about the individual's request for help. Is it believable? Are any key facts missing? Is there a tremendous amount of detail—in order to convince you—that is irrelevant to the main point of his or her story? Has the person "forgotten" key information, given only partial answers to your questions, or tried to change the subject? Is he or she demanding immediate action so you won't have time to consider the request? Is the needy person trying to make you feel guilty for doubting his or her honesty?

3. Follow every possible alternative to giving money. If you decide to give money, settle on a firm amount, and don't allow him or her to change your mind.

TRANSIENTS

Sometimes the church may be called on to help transient people who don't have the proper resources to get from one place to another.

Common items needed by transients:

Food—An Elijah's Barrel, or a church pantry to which members donate food items, can help meet this need, or arrangements can be made with a local restaurant to provide hot meals.

Lodging—Arrangements can be made with a motel or hotel to provide lodging.

Bus fare—Set an amount for the purchase of bus tickets. The ticket should help the person reach another location where more help can be found.

COUNSELING PROGRAM

Church welfare programs need an excellent counseling program, operated by qualified lay persons—not the pastor, who is generally too busy to do financial counseling and is usually not trained for the job.

Counselors need to be trained thoroughly and properly. Christian Financial Concepts offers a training program for counselors within the local church and will be glad to supply more information.

RESOURCES

Christians desiring to start a church welfare program should be aware of the resources within their local churches. Not only do they need the financial support of other believers to help meet legitimate needs, but they need physical help to screen families, deliver food, and get them started on the road to being productive members of the church and community.

Paul says in 2 Corinthians 8:14 to share with those in need in your time of plenty, that in your time of need they will be willing to share from their plenty.

Jobs. First, find sources for available jobs. One church selected five individuals to be trained as financial counselors and sent them to Christian Financial Concepts' seminars on biblical principles of handling money.

Afterward, they were trained to counsel and went through Christian Financial Concepts' "Teacher Training Workshop." When they finished, they were equipped to begin financial counseling with couples or individuals who were having problems.

But then they had to find their resources. Where were the available jobs? In this case it was a fairly large church, and they set up a job program.

In fact, they started a building program, so when unemployed people came for help they were hired to help with the building. They actually hammered, sawed, and painted under the supervision of a trained lay person. The money had been donated by others within the local church, not only to employ people but to actually build the building.

They also found Christians within their fellowship who had businesses that needed part-time help. One was a mailing service that always needed part-time help, and another was a parking service. Although these jobs paid only $4 an hour, that was $4 an hour less that the church needed to provide.

Maintain a list of church construction or work projects that can provide income for qualified people. Also keep a list of businesspeople who will provide part-time or permanent jobs.

Surplus funds and goods. Another important factor in church welfare is locating sources of surplus funds for temporary needs, because many people have only temporary needs. They might have an illness or disability that keeps them from working for a period of time.

There must be a resource of goods. Some churches have started Elijah's Barrels, to which other believers within the church donate food, clothes, and toys for the specific purpose of distributing to needy families who have gone through counseling.

Standby activities. Also needed are standby activities, such as auto maintenance. One church invites single women, particularly older women, to come once per month to the church parking lot and have maintenance done on their cars. Their cars are tuned up, the oil is changed, and so on. Many of the women can't afford to keep their cars running properly. The men doing the maintenance are church members ranging from veterinarians to attorneys.

Individuals also can offer help in their own professions. Needy people often cannot afford legal or accounting advice or medical and dental care. The benevolence committee should be made aware of all persons desiring to contribute their services or time and maintain a current list of names and contributions.

WHERE DOES IT BEGIN?

Church benevolence programs begin with one individual who says, "I believe God called me to do that." If that person is you, don't hesitate to start such a program in your church. It takes a first step. It takes someone saying, "I am going to do something to help my church meet the needs of people—first, within my own local body and, second, within my community."

To acquire the knowledge needed to set up the benevolence committee, a clothes closet, or Elijah's Barrel, someone needs to be trained. And someone also needs to be trained to do financial counseling.

The only way to do it is simply to get started. One of the purposes of Christian Financial Concepts is to help people get started. The next step is to gather a group of people with the same concern who are willing to care for truly needy people. There are enough people out there who care, if only one person will organize them.

Usually when such committees get started

they are overwhelmed with help. The church becomes known as a "caring church," and the word gets out that if you don't have a legitimate need, don't go there because they put you through a screening process and make you work.

To start a benevolence program you must commit time and money. Don't ask others to do what you are not willing to do yourself. Approach your pastor and the leadership of your church with a clear plan.

One individual was so convicted about starting a welfare program that he opened a used clothing store, which is now a thrift shop, where he employed unemployable people. When people come to his church, which is noted for being a "caring church," and say, "I cannot find a job. I have looked to the best of my ability, and I am willing to take whatever is available," he always has a job in his store. He does it as a ministry, not as a business.

The Bible tells us to share with those who are in need in our time of plenty. Believe what Christ said, and believe it to the extent that you do it "to the least of these" in your community, regardless of whether they are saved, and especially to those within your own church. Remember that as you serve others you also serve Christ.

CHRISTIAN FUND-RAISING

Fund-raising would seem the national pastime of most nonprofit organizations in America today. According to the bulk of mail received by most Christian givers, there is little doubt that competition for Christian support is acute. New organizations spring up every day, and as the number of organizations grows, the search for new funds becomes more intense, as anyone who has donated money to one or more general-appeal groups knows. After one donation, almost mystically an unsuspecting donor receives requests from scores of other unknown organizations. That is because many organizations either use a common fund-raising company or they sell their donor lists to generate additional income.

Many well-meaning Christians get pressured into giving to groups they know little or nothing about because of emotional appeals or skilled manipulation.

Many otherwise sound Christian ministries have turned to secular advertising and fund-raising companies to meet their growing demand for funds. Often they pay up to 40 percent of all donations just to raise more money. Some promoters actually work on fund-raising campaigns for anti-Christian and Christian groups simultaneously. All this is to say that we must be responsible for how the money God has entrusted to us is used.

Before supporting any fund appeal, we should ask some basic questions.

WHO?

Who is the group asking for the funds? Get a list of references from the organization that can be easily verified through other well-known groups. It would be wise to write a letter to the attorney general of the state of residence and also a letter to the head of a ministry or church nearby. Often the best method is to do it through your own pastor or church secretary.

WHAT?

What are they going to use the funds for? One good way to determine this is to ask for a projected budget. (The lack of a budget is one reason many organizations continually send out "crisis appeal" letters.)

HOW?

How do they raise funds, and how do they manage them? It is wise to ask if a fund-raising company is involved and what percentage of the funds go to them. Also, how much of the ministry's budget is dedicated to fund-raising? Obviously some media ministries (radio and TV) would have a higher portion dedicated to raising money. A good indication of financial management is the debt to income ratio and the change in overhead expenses from year to year.

Once those questions are asked, the burden of

making the decision based on common sense is satisfied. However, the burden of exercising spiritual wisdom can only be satisfied by the application of God's Word.

BIBLICAL PRINCIPLES

There must be a balance in a Christian's attitude toward ministry support. Often an individual reads a spectacular biography of how God used a particular person and uses that as an absolute rule against everyone else. Personal testimonies are exciting and rewarding and can be of great value in providing alternatives. However, they are not to be used as yardsticks, unless they are confirmed in God's Word. For example, many Christians have read the story of George Mueller's life and how he trusted God for everything without asking anyone. They conclude that no Christian should ever let a material need be known. That is noble and admirable, but it is not scriptural. Paul admonished the Corinthians because they thought he didn't have the right to ask them for support (2 Corinthians 11:7-9). In Exodus 25:1-3 the Lord tells Moses to tell the people of Israel to raise a contribution for the tabernacle.

On the other hand, just because asking is acceptable doesn't mean that it's God's plan for everyone or that every letter sent to supporters should ask for more money. Again, balance is the key. Nowhere in Scripture is there any indication that God's people went begging. It would appear that many more needs were met by praying than by asking. It also seems clear that once God's people are made aware of their responsibilities to give and support God's work, the need to ask would go down dramatically (Exodus 36:5-6).

WHICH GROUPS TO SUPPORT?

God does not intend for every Christian to give to every need. Attempting to do so would quickly result in frustration and, for most of us, poverty. Therefore, we must be able to distinguish those we are to help from those we aren't.

GOD'S WORK

There are many worthy social organizations serving the needs of the poor, the sick, and the elderly. The vast majority make no pretense of working in the name of the Lord. That should exclude them from receiving the portion set apart for God. It is abundantly clear throughout the Bible that gifts dedicated to God were to be distributed in His name. Since God obviously did not need the material goods, they were redistributed to satisfy those who had needs (see Exodus 34:19; Leviticus 1:2, 27:30; Deuteronomy 12:6, 14:28).

DESERVING

Even if a group has an emotional presentation for a seemingly worthy Christian cause, that does not mean they automatically qualify for support. It is important to determine that the funds will actually be used for the purpose stated.

Above all else, be certain about the doctrinal stand of the ministry. Many committed believers are shocked to discover that they are contributing to an organization that is anti-Christian.

PERSONAL BENEFIT

Organizations that have met needs in your life should be high on your support list. Obviously, the people most supportive of a ministry should be the ones it has ministered to. If the organization is not highly visible (does not advertise or make regular appeals), the support of those they have helped is essential. *"Let the one who is taught the word share all good things with him who teaches"* (Galatians 6:6).

GOOD STEWARDS

Just as in any other investment, Christians should get the best benefit of their investments in God's work. So the organizations that manage their funds the best should be considered first. Obviously, the type of ministry a group is involved in must also be considered. For example, a rural church and a national television ministry will have vastly different budgets and should not be evaluated by total expenditures. If you have a desire to support a particular type of ministry, locate the most efficient and productive one available.

The leaders of any ministry should have a clear, concise plan for accomplishing God's work and a reasonable idea of costs and time. The lack of written goals and objectives is usually a sign of slothfulness. There are other signs to look for, such as a heavy debt burden, bad credit history, unfinished projects, significant staff turnover, and soliciting support from the unsaved.

"I passed by the field of the sluggard, and by the vineyard of the man lacking sense; and behold, it was completely overgrown with thistles" (Proverbs 24:30-31). (See also 1 Corinthians 9:14; Luke 16:13.)

GOD'S LEADING

The most important principle of all is to allow God to direct your giving. We are told to lean upon God's wisdom and not our own understanding (Proverbs 3:5), and that also applies to giving. Anyone who has a problem turning down requests must learn to wait and pray before giving. If your problem is not wanting to give to anyone, you need to give more and wait less. *"Whoever has the world's goods, and beholds his brother in need and closes his heart against him, how does the love of God abide in him?"* (1 John 3:17).

An essential part of the balance system God has established is the husband and wife relationship. Almost without exception, one partner is prone to give too much and the other too little.

Couples who learn to communicate and accept each other's counsel usually establish a reasonable balance.

GUIDELINES

It is impossible to lay down absolute guidelines for funding God's work because God did not do so in His Word. However, there are some good guidelines available for both askers and givers. Givers would be well advised to use biblical guidelines whenever possible in selecting organizations to give to. Then rely on God's inner direction to decide which groups to support. Use these biblical guidelines for each organization.

1. Adhering to sound biblical doctrine in the organization and ministry (Galatians 1:9)

2. Ministering in the name of the Lord Jesus Christ (Colossians 3:17)

3. Practicing of good financial management within the organization (Luke 16:12)

4. Depending on God's people for support (John 3:6-7)

5. Changing lives for Christ through the ministry (Galatians 5:22-23)

An organization that investigates and reports financial responsibility in ministries is ECFA (Economic Council for Financial Accountability) PO Box 17456, Washington DC 20041-0456

Top Resources From Larry Burkett

How to Manage Your Money

This newly re-packaged bestseller contains
updated material, plus a step-by-step, in-depth
study of God's principles for money
management.

More than 700,000 Sold!

ISBN: 0-8024-1476-1, Workbook

Top Resources From Larry Burkett

Family Financial Workbook

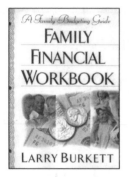

Includes every easy-to-follow worksheet you need to structure and maintain your family's budget. Contains extra worksheets so you can go back year after year.

More than 600,000 sold as *The Financial Planning Workbook*

ISBN: 0-8024-1475-3, Workbook